pseud Gérôme

Christ and the Critics

pseud Gérôme

Christ and the Critics

ISBN/EAN: 9783337022525

Printed in Europe, USA, Canada, Australia, Japan

Cover: Foto ©Lupo / pixelio.de

More available books at **www.hansebooks.com**

Christ
and
The Critics

By
GÉRÔME

Cincinnati: Curts & Jennings
New York: Eaton & Mains
1898

Contents

	PAGE
PREFACE,	5

CHAPTER I
THE CASE IN COURT, - - - - 7

CHAPTER II
THE APPEAL TO THE MASTER, - 18

CHAPTER III
DID MOSES WRITE THE PENTATEUCH, 40

CHAPTER IV
MOSES AND THE BOOKS, - - 51

CHAPTER V
RECONCILIATION, - - - - 73

Preface

A glance at these few pages will show that no attempt has been made to solve any philological, geographical, historical, theological, or other question of Higher Criticism. None of the supposed inaccuracies, discrepancies, or contradictions pointed out by radical critics have been touched. I did not design to do so. Holding all these matters for the time being in abeyance, I have sought the answer to one question only, *and that was, not what the Old Testament books said as to their authorship, not what the apostles and evangelists said, not what the voices of the ages have said, but* what did Christ say? *All other questions, except the authorship of the Pentateuch, remain as they are. But the settlement of this one question will enable earnest students to approach difficulties with less fear.*

The final chapter is added for the simple purpose of showing that the conclusions reached are not inimical to the noble results of modern scholarship.

GÉRÔME.

Christ and the Critics

CHAPTER I

The Case in Court

IN the National Gallery of Fine Arts in Berlin there hangs, or did hang, a famous picture by Kaulbach, representing a battle of the Huns before the gates of Rome. What is remarkable in the painting, aside from its drawing and color, is the bold conception of the artist in depicting the souls of the combatants as rising, quick with wrath, from the mingled heaps of the slain, and continuing the awful conflict in the air.

Some such scene floats before the mind when one contemplates the battle that is now being fought around the sacred Scriptures.

The combatants die in the struggle, but in their writings, which live after them, they still urge on the warring hosts, and still strive for the triumph of their views.

The question before the court of Christian belief is: Were the books of the Bible originally written by those to whom they are credited? This is the issue that divides now the Christian scholarship of the world. The case is a difficult one, and is contested with energy by opposing counsel. An imposing array of Biblical scholars, both in Europe and America, eminent as specialists in their several lines of research, affirm that these books were not written by those whose names they bear. Moses did not write the Pentateuch, nor any book in it. Joshua was not written at, nor near the time of the events which it narrates, but long after—some 800 or 700 years before the time of Christ. Not all of Isaiah, but only a few chapters, were composed by that prophet. All of that book bearing his name, from chapter xl to chapter lxvi inclusive, is of unknown authorship, and was written at the close of the Exile. The Psalms have their origin also, according to some critics, in a Post-exilic period, even as late as the days of the Maccabees. David wrote a few of them, but other poets wrote the most important ones. Thus every book almost of the Old Testament is asserted to be the work, not of the writer who has been believed both by Jew and Christian to have been the author, but of some unknown editors who for pious purposes gathered up various narratives, prophecies, and historical fragments, and dovetailed them with more or less skill and accuracy into a connected whole; thus making the Old Testament as we now have it.

This seems to be a very bold treatment of our historic faith, and to those unacquainted with the evidence in the case it may seem to be a very weak and futile attempt of rationalism to undermine the authority of the Holy Scriptures. But the conclusions above stated are based upon the principles of Higher Criticism. Higher Criticism is a literary science. As applied to the Bible its object is the verification of all the data, philological, historical, or other, relating to the origin, genuineness, and authenticity of the Scriptural books. The methods of this science are various. The principal ones, or those chiefly employed to determine the date, authorship, theology, or unity of a document, are three: The Literary, the Historical, and the Theological, with their several divisions.

THE LITERARY METHOD.—Every document discloses certain literary characteristics of its author. These earmarks include the use of synonyms, figures of speech, fondness for idioms, peculiar words, tone, color, everything that constitutes *style*, and enriches or impoverishes its quality. No two writers, perhaps, have equal power over language, either in the arrangement, or in the precision, or in the number of the words employed. And, again, a close study of an author will reveal the vocabulary familiar to him, and which he constantly employs. Canon Driver, in his *Introduction to the Literature of the Old Testament*, gives long lists of characteristic phrases in

Deuteronomy which are not found in other portions of the Pentateuch. Dr. Charles A. Briggs supplies another list of words used in some parts of a book, but which are not found in other parts of the same book. Then, further, in the same book there may be discernible a difference of style. One part is poetic and descriptive; another is analytical, showing the predominance of the logical faculty; while another part is rhetorical, or carefully avoids any suggestion of color or imagery, being severely chaste and prosaically solid.

These peculiarities of language and variations of style, analyzed and grouped according to established principles of literary criticism, lead to the conclusion that when these different characteristics are seen in a document, that document is not the product of one writer. More than one has left the impress of his genius on that particular work.

THE HISTORICAL METHOD.—As writings reveal the literary ability and characteristics of an author, so also do they reflect the history of the times in which they were written. No writer on themes intended to influence human conduct can be wholly impervious to the play of the political, social, or religious forces of his own day. Some trace of their movement, some effect of their influence on the writer himself, will crop out somewhere in his work. Literature is the mirror of history. Works containing references to the telegraph, the phonograph, or the telephone, could not by any possibility be accredited to the age of Augustus or to the days of Shakespeare and Elizabeth. For instance, in Genesis xxxvi, 31, we read these strange words, "And these are the kings that reigned in the land of Edom *before there reigned any king over the children of Israel.*" This last statement forces one, it would seem, to the conclusion that that portion of Genesis could not have been written at the date usually assigned to the Book of Genesis, but must have been composed *after* the monarchy had been instituted in Israel. Again, in Genesis xiv, 14, we read: "And pursued them unto Dan." But the name "Dan," we are informed elsewhere (Judges xviii, 29), was not given to this place till long after the time of Moses, and therefore, it is argued, this portion of Genesis is the product of a later hand than the hand of Moses. Thus it is seen writings of importance, especially if the writers were involved in the movements of their time, and were in any degree impressed by changing events and the operation of complex forces about them, may readily be assigned by the methods of historical criticism to their respective periods.

THE THEOLOGICAL METHOD.—Theology is progressive. The religious development of a nation follows the same general law of progress observable in the evolution of society, manners, morals, and government. All development, as Herbert Spencer has shown, is from the homogeneous to the heteregeneous, from the simple to the complex, through successive differentiations. But in the Pentateuch there is a scheme of religion, a system of theology, an elaborateness and complexity of ritual, that could not have been possible until the nation had passed through successive stages of culture and had reached a high degreee of development. It is utterly unscientific, because contrary to experience, to attribute to an elementary stage in national growth, ideas and conditions that belong, and can belong only, to an advanced period.

By application of this method to the Pentateuch, the result is that Deuteronomy, Leviticus, and portions of Genesis must be credited to other times than those of Moses. The manner in which Divine revelation was communicated differs in divers places in the Pentateuch; the conception of miracles differs, as does also the doctrine of the covenants. The doctrine of the Holy Spirit shows great development between Genesis x, 21, 38, and Exodus xxxi, 3. The same may be concluded relative to the Divine attributes, to the doctrine of holiness, the doctrine of sin, and the teaching with regard to redemption.

Such are the methods of Higher Criticism. To every book of the Bible these principles are applied with scientific rigor, and no document is accepted that can not stand the test. The result is, that scarcely a scholar of note in Germany or in England now maintains the traditional view of the origin of our sacred books. What shall we do?—surrender the belief of the ages? If to possess the truth it is necessary to do so, then it becomes our duty to accept the conclusions of the critics without regard to consequences. But before we surrender, we will first discover the necessity.

CHAPTER II

The Appeal to the Master

IN opposition to the findings of radical critics, the old belief still holds the field. Old faiths are not easily dug up: their roots are many, widely ramified, and deeply imbedded. The traditional view, modified by scholars of no mean ability, is based on internal and external proofs, and the methods of the radicals are as honestly employed by the conservatives in reaching conclusions which, notwithstanding the brilliant array of eminent names in Biblical science opposed to them, have not yet been demonstrated to be weak enough to be abandoned. The discoveries in the mounds of Babylonia and Nineveh are adding strength to the positions of the conservatives, and it is believed that the pick and spade will yet dig the grave of many an ultra-radical theory.

But the conflict continues. Christian men are disturbed—they scarcely know what to think; and between the antagonists, of which neither will surrender to the other, who shall decide? Is there no tribunal, no court of last resort, no judge or authority, to whom we can go, and no matter how difficult it may be to reconcile his verdict with the results of modern scholarship, still feel abiding confidence in his judgment? There is.

Conservative critics appeal to the Great Teacher, the Lord Jesus. This is the most natural thing in the world for Christians to do; provided the Lord has spoken or can be appealed to. But radical critics object. The moment an appeal is made to Christ, the air is full of objections and demurrers of every description. Dr. Charles A. Briggs meets the appeal to our Lord in this manner:

"Why should we interpret Jesus and his apostles by the opinions of the Jews of his time? Why should we suppose that he shared with them all the errors he did not oppose and refute? Jesus either knew that Moses wrote the Pentateuch or not. If we should say that Jesus did not know whether Moses wrote the Pentateuch or not, we would not go beyond his own saying that he did not know the time of his own advent. Those who understand the doctrine of the humiliation of Christ and the incarnation of Christ, find no more difficulty in supposing that Jesus did not know the author of the Pentateuch than that he did not know the day of his own advent." (*The Higher Criticism of the Pentateuch*, p. 29.)

Professor Charles Gore also says:

"When he [our Lord] speaks of the 'sun rising,' he is using ordinary language. He shows no signs at all of transcending the science of his age. . . . The utterances of Christ about the Old Testament do not seem to be nearly definite or clear enough to allow of our supposing that in this case he is departing from the general method of the incarnation by bringing to bear the unveiled omniscience of the Godhead to anticipate or foreclose a development of natural knowledge."

And Canon Driver, in his truly great work (*Introduction to the Literature of the Old Testament;* Preface, xiv), says:

"That our Lord appealed to the Old Testament as the record of a revelation in the past, and as pointing forward to himself, is undoubted; but these aspects of the Old Testament are perfectly consistent with a critical view of its structure and growth. . . . He accepted, as the basis of his teaching, the opinions respecting the Old Testament current around him. . . . There is no record of the question whether a particular portion of the Old Testament was written by Moses, or David, or Isaiah, ever having been submitted to him; and had it been so submitted, we have no means of knowing what his answer would have been."

Shall these demurrers of the critics be allowed? If so, there can be no appeal, and the case must be given up. But we do not think there is anything in the unsupported statements of these critics necessarily sustaining their case. Each one of them assumes the whole question in his statement. Professor Briggs asks, "Why should we interpret Jesus and his apostles by the opinions of the Jews of his time?" as if any competent person ever did so. Of all weak modes of argument, the weakest is to attribute to an opponent opinions he does not hold. No one imagines that Jesus shared in every error of his day which he did not refute. Not to refute an error, however, but to acquiesce in and affirm it, and to make that error one's own as the basis of teaching any truth, physical or moral, are two very different things, with the width of a world between them. It is a fact that between the opinions of his time relative to the authorship of the Old Testament and the expressed views of Jesus there is full agreement. But what evidence is there in that that these opinions were erroneous, or that our Lord simply accepted them without knowing them to be such, or regarded such opinions as having no material relation to his teaching?

As to the opinion, shared alike

by Dr. Briggs and Professor Gore, that because of the limitations inherent in the humiliation of our Lord in the incarnation he did not know who wrote the Pentateuch, this may be said: That such an opinion assumes to know too much of the character and extent of those limitations. There are times in the life of our Lord when he seems to have no limitations except such as he voluntarily, consciously maintains. More than once his omniscience manifests itself, as in the case of Nathanael, in his knowledge of the death of Lazarus, and in his knowledge of a coin in the mouth of a fish. Whatever view we may hold of the humiliation of our Lord— whether it be that of Delitzsch, Kahnis, or König; of Reuss, Godet, or Hoffman; or of any other student of this awful mystery,—

there is one granite-rock truth not to be forgotten, and that is, *Our Lord never laid aside or lost his God-consciousness.* He always knows his identity with Him who was not man, but became man. He is always conscious of his continuity as the same One who relinquished the form of God and became flesh.

Now, Jesus knew, or he did not know, who wrote the Pentateuch. If he did not know, then he could not have known that *Moses* had written of him, as he said he had. If he did not know *that*, then how could our Lord have expressly declared that *Moses did write* concerning him? It will not do to evade this difficulty by assuming that Christ's statement was an interpretation of the writings attributed to Moses. There is no bending, no accommodation, to common belief here. The whole context shows that he is on a higher plane. He does not say, "In the Scriptures," or "In the books ascribed to Moses," nor does he use any term indicating any book or number of books under a general title which would leave the question of authorship still undetermined; but on a special occasion, and for *a specific purpose*, he places, beyond all ambiguity of language, the authorship of a Messianic passage on a distinct personality—on *Moses*, the lawgiver of Israel. It is difficult to believe that Christ would have said Moses wrote of him if Moses had not written of him, and if he knew that Moses had not so written. Christ knew whether he was speaking from personal knowledge or according to the common belief of his time; and if he, with his contemporaries, was mistaken in the authorship of the Pentateuch, by what means shall it be proved that he was not mistaken also in its interpretation?

Between the ability to interpret the Scriptures and the knowing who wrote any particular book there may seem to be no sort of connection. One may be able, it will be said, to explain correctly what is written without being able to prove who made the writing. That is true; and it is also true that one may be mistaken in his explanation, since he can not affirm that his interpretation is infallible, and from his error no great injurious result may follow. But it is not so with Jesus Christ. His interpretation must be infallible; otherwise he would not be the Truth nor the Way. But the fact that Moses wrote Scripture *is itself a question of interpretation;* for it is recorded that Moses wrote certain things—Ex. xxiv, 4; Num. xxiii, 2; Deut. xxxi, 9; 1 Kings viii, 9; 2 Chron. xxxiii, 8; Neh. ix, 14; and in numerous other places—so that when our Lord says Moses was the author of any book, or of any law in any book which by implication would make him the author of that book, he is not depending for his statement on the opinions of the Jews of his time, or of any time. *Back of his statement is the authority of Holy Scripture and his own infallible interpretation of that Scripture.* He knew the truth. He understood the Scriptures as no one else did or could understand them. This knowledge he imparted to his disciples: "And beginning from Moses and from all the prophets, he *interpreted* to them in all the Scriptures the things concerning himself." (Luke xxiv, 27.)

A very interesting bit of evidence in proof, under all the circumstances, that Moses had written of the Christ, and that Christ had personal knowledge of that fact, is seen in the narrative, overlooked by our critics, of the conversation between Christ and Moses on the Mount of Transfiguration. Here Christ is in direct personal communication with Moses. The Evangelist Luke says: "And behold there talked with him two men, which were Moses and Elias, who appeared in glory, and spake of his decease [exodus], which he should accomplish at Jerusalem." The subject of the discourse is Christ's death. And let it be carefully observed here that our Lord is not giving information *to* Moses or *to* Elias—

they already know what is to happen; but they are talking *to him*, and the subject is his approaching death at Jerusalem. They know Christ, and they know his mission. Christ certainly knows them, and that all three perfectly understand that there is common knowledge among them of something definite and important about to take place, is an irresistible impression springing immediately from a reading of the narrative.

Try as we may to get away from this conviction, we can no more shake it off than one can escape from his shadow; for the moment we read the narrative, we intuitively apprehend that it must be so.

Now, Christ had declared to the Jews that Moses had written concerning him: "For had ye believed Moses, ye would have believed me; for he wrote of me. But if ye believe not his writings, how shall ye believe my words?" (John v, 46, 47.) But where had Moses written concerning Christ if not in the Pentateuch, in Genesis, and in Deuteronomy, which last Canon Driver puts long after the age of Moses? In Genesis it is written: "I will put enmity between thee and the woman, and between thy seed and her seed: it shall bruise thy head, and thou shalt bruise his heel." All Biblical scholars of high repute recognize this passage as truly Messianic—Delitzsch, Orelli, Lange, Oehler, to mention no more. Is there no connection, then, between this writing attributed to Moses and the conversation between Moses and Christ concerning *his death?* We can not say the same with reference to Elias, who was also present and took part in the conference; for the circumstances are not the same. Elias wrote nothing, and our Lord never referred to him as authority in his teaching. But, given the subject of the conversation with Moses, the *death* of Christ; given the fact that Christ said that Moses *wrote* of him; and given also the fact that in Genesis, which was attributed to Moses, the suffering of the Coming One is predicted,—does it not look very much as if Moses really did write the Book of Genesis, and, which is the point now, *that Christ knew that he had written it?*

Professor Gore objects because it would be an "unveiling of Omniscience." Well, suppose it was, what of that? But is it any more an "unveiling of Omniscience" for Christ to know that Moses wrote the Pentateuch, than it was for Moses to know that Christ was about to suffer and die at Jerusalem? or, than it was that Christ should foretell the destruction of the Holy City, see Nathanael under the fig-tree, see a coin in the mouth of a fish, or know that that particular fish would so direct its movements in the water that it would be caught by Peter?

Again our Lord said, "Abraham rejoiced to see my day, and was glad." *How did Christ know that?* It is nowhere written in Scripture. If we say that it was an inference drawn by Christ from the recorded promise to Abraham, that in his seed all the nations of the earth should be blessed, we are only saying that Christ so interpreted that Scripture as to make it applicable to himself. But, observe, if Christ had absolute knowledge, infallible perception, that that Scripture referred to him personally, could he not have had the same infallible perception, with or without "unveiling of Omniscience," that when the Scriptures said expressly that Moses wrote the Book of the Law or any other writing, Moses really did write what was attributed to him, and not some one else who was not Moses? If Christ could have known, outside of any expressed record in Scripture, what Abraham *felt* hundreds of years before Moses was born, could he not as easily have known whether or not Moses wrote the Pentateuch?

The statement of Canon Driver, which we may now consider, is also insufficient, we think, to sustain the demurrer to our appeal to the Master. It is of no greater strength, when analyzed, than the objections of Professor Briggs or of Canon Gore, and the opinion of this eminent critic must be considered in the light of all the statements and teachings of the Master. For example, our Lord based his claims to being the Messiah on the authority of God's Scriptures. Not wholly and absolutely so, it is true; but he rested his claims on these enough to justify the statement. From the judgments of his critics concerning his claims he appealed to the Scriptures; for said he, "They testify of me." Prophecies relating to the Messiah dated back, it was firmly believed by the whole nation, to the very dawn of Israel's beginning, and even back to the morning of time. Christ himself believed that; he most certainly traced Messianic predictions as far back as the remote age of Abraham;

for referring to the promise of Jehovah to Abraham, recorded in Genesis, the Book of the Beginnings, he said, "Abraham rejoiced to see my day, and was glad."

But if modern expounders and defenders of radical Higher Criticism are correct in their conclusions, this belief was a baseless belief. Moreover, this hope of the earliest ages in a Messiah of the future must be abandoned—they had no such millennium dreams; for none of the books in which this prophecy of a Messiah is recorded were written at the time or near the time, nor by the divinely commissioned persons they were believed to have been written by, but in other ages long after, under other social and religious conditions, and by authors unknown—unknown in the Scriptures themselves, and unknown to the nation to whom the Scriptures came. Are we prepared to admit that Christ built his Messianic claims on a false foundation, on a baseless legend?

Our Lord teaches, beyond any chance for mistaken exegesis, that the Messiah was predicted in the Books of Moses. But the critics insist that the Books of Moses were not in existence in the days of Moses, that they are the product of a later stage of national development. Are we then to believe that Christ was mistaken?

Canon Driver can hardly expect Christian men to accept that conclusion; and yet, no matter how much he might strive, by modifying phrases and verbal limitations, to soften its startling harshness, it is the only logical conclusion permissible. When we are informed on the authority of Oxford scholarship that our Lord " accepted as the basis of his teaching the opinions respecting the Old Testament current around him "—we require some proof for the statement, if by it is meant that our Lord himself had any other opinion.

Jesus was a teacher. True, he did not come to teach science, archæology, or literary criticism; but he was, nevertheless, a *true teacher;* he did not teach truth on a false basis. He did believe and teach the antiquity of the Mosaic books, and if his opinions coincided with the opinions "current around him," this militates not against those opinions, but against the assumptions of Canon Driver. In view then of all the facts in the case, briefly stated, we see no reason why we may not appeal to the Master for a solution of the question between the opposing schools of Biblical criticism. To the words of the Master we have appealed, we think we are justified in doing so, and to the Master we now go.

CHAPTER III

Did Moses Write the Pentateuch?

TO THE Master we have appealed, and to him we have come. Our appeal is not as to the Divine character of the sacred books. That question is settled for us by the Lord Jesus in the New Testament: For the *Book of Genesis*, by Matt. x, 4-8; xxiv, 37-39; Mark x, 4-9; Luke xi, 40-51; John viii, 44. For the *Book of Exodus*, by Matt. iv, 7, 12; xii, 3-5; xxii, 31, 32; Mark vii, 9, 10; x, 19; John vi, 31-49. For the *Book of Leviticus*, by Mark i, 44; John vi, 31-49; xxii, 23. For *Numbers*, by John iii, 14; vi, 31-49. For *Deuteronomy*, by Matt. iv, 4, 7, 10; Mark x, 4-9. And for all the *Old Testament books*, by Matt. v, 7; xi, 13; xxvi, 54; Luke xxiv; John v, 29; xix, 28.

But the question we propose is: Did Moses write any of the books of the Bible? Dr. Briggs teaches that Moses wrote a few fragments only in the Pentateuch, such as Exodus xx, 22–26; xxi–xxiii; the Ten Commandments, the Code in Deuteronomy xii–xxvi, possibly a song (Deut. xxi, 32), and the list of the stages in the march of Israel from Egypt to the Jordan Valley.

This is all that Moses wrote. Canon Driver, while believing that the Song of Moses was handed down from an early period, assigns the date of incorporating it into Deuteronomy to a time when Israel had already possessed Canaan. According to him, Deuteronomy was not written by Moses, but by some unknown, who introduces him in the third person. It was written, he thinks, prior to the eighteenth year of King Josiah, B. C. 621. The Mosaic authorship of Genesis can not, he says, be sustained.

Driver agrees in the main with Professor Briggs, Cheyne, Robertson Smith, C. H. Toy, and the advocates of what is known among the critics as the Grafian School. The view distinguishing this school from other schools of Biblical criticism is: (1) The Five Books of Moses and the Book of Joshua constitute one work, the Hexateuch. (2) This entire work originated thus: An unknown writer, named J, because of his use of the word Jehovah, composed a history of the Israelites about the year 800 B. C. He had some material, derived from an earlier day, which formed the basis of his work. (3) Some fifty years later—B. C. 750—another historian, designated E, from his use of the word Elohim, wrote a similar book. At the end of the seventh century before Christ, these two books, J and E, were made over, by an unknown editor, into one book. (4) Later, another writer, named D, wrote, about the time of King Josiah—621 B. C.—the Book of Deuteronomy. Some one added a preface to this book, and after a time another editor joined it to the previous books J E. (5) During the days of the Prophet Ezekiel, the Ritual Law was written, and appeared in three forms. Ezra reduced these laws, about 444 B. C., to one code; and, by another editor, the codified laws were united with the books J E D, somewhere between that date and 280 B. C.

Such was the origin of the

Five Books of Moses and the Book of Joshua, now named the Hexateuch. Evidently, Moses had very little to do with the composition of the Pentateuch. But what does Christ say? In the Gospel according to John, chapter v, there are recorded some very clear words of our Lord bearing on this subject. In his controversy with the leaders of his day, he said:

> Do not think that I will accuse you to the Father; there is one that accuseth you, even Moses, in whom ye trust. For had ye believed Moses, ye would have believed me: for he wrote of me. But if ye believe not his writings, how shall ye believe my words?

How is it possible to reconcile these words with the statements of the critics? Moses will accuse; but on what ground will Moses accuse? He wrote but a fragment here and there of the Law, and that Law was their national life, which they strove to maintain. We can not say that Christ meant by "Moses" the books of Moses. The record will not allow that. It is a passage of contrasts—a contrast of persons and of "words" over against "writings." The leaders trusted in an individual, in *a person*, Moses. But they were deceiving themselves. In reality they were opposed to Moses. Antagonism to Christ was antagonism to Moses; for he wrote of Christ as the One who should come *like* him. They were, in opposing Christ, opposing the *person*, not a figurative personality, but the *individual*, Moses. How could that be, if Moses was *not*, in a real material sense, the author of writings concerning the Christ? Wherein did they oppose *him*, and on what ground could *he* accuse *them?*

Our Lord says Moses wrote of

him. We must find Christ, then, in the books attributed to Moses. But where, in those fragments which some critics ascribe to Moses, do we find anything pertaining to Christ? Professor Briggs concedes that Exodus xx, 22–26, was written by Moses; but Christ is not there. Exodus xxi–xxiii is also assigned to Moses; but Christ is not there. Moses wrote the Ten Commandments; but no coming Christ is there. Where, then, in the writings ascribed to Moses by the critics, shall we find the Christ? Truly, one might exclaim, "They have taken away my Lord, and I know not where they have laid him!" The Code of Laws—Deut. xii–xxvi—is conceded to be the authorship of Moses; but in all these chapters there is only *one verse* which is capable of being interpreted as referring to the Lord Jesus: "The

Lord thy God will raise up unto thee a prophet from the midst of thee, of thy brethren, like unto me: unto him ye shall hearken." (Deut. xviii, 15. See the 18th verse.)

Out of all the writings, then, which the critics allow Moses, we find only *one solitary verse* relating to Christ, and that one verse, with its repetition, is in a book which Driver and others assign to the period of the monarchy!

Now is it reasonable to suppose that when our Lord said, "Had ye believed Moses, ye would have believed me: for he wrote of me. But if ye believe not his writings, how shall ye believe my words?" that by the "writings" he meant *one* verse? But this solitary passage is all that is written concerning the Messiah anywhere in those Scriptures which the critics affirm were all the Scriptures that Moses actually wrote.

In the light, then, of the Master's own words, what is the natural conclusion? This: The critics are mistaken. In the nature of the case, Moses must have written more than the critics allow him. Christ says Moses "wrote of"—concerning—him. Christ is not in what the critics say Moses wrote; therefore Christ was mistaken, or else Moses wrote more than the critics grant. The question, then, as we see it, narrows itself to this: Which is mistaken, Christ or the critics?

The conclusion to which we have come may be at war with all the results of Biblical criticism; it may be distasteful to those critics who have bestowed great labor, guided by learned skill, in constructing their theories: but we are not to be frightened at that. Criticism itself may be in need of criticism. Theories are valuable, not according to the learning or ingenuity displayed in their structure, but in proportion to the measure of truth they contain.

It should be observed, also, that Christ's condemnation of the Pharisees and scribes before him was based on the understood fact that Moses was the author of "*writings*" which they falsely professed to believe. Too much stress can not be placed upon this; for if the books of Moses were *not* the "writings" of Moses, but the work of unknown editors, where was the point or the significance of our Lord's question, "If ye believe not *his writings*, how shall ye believe *my words?*" Certainly one might formulate some sort of a reply, such as that the hopeless character of these men whom Jesus addressed was just as real if Moses was not the author of the Pentateuch; for they professed to follow what they did not follow. But such a reply evades the real force of the contrast in Christ's question — "*his writings*," "*my words*." Christ does not put his person as the Messiah of God against, or alongside of, a fiction.

CHAPTER IV

Moses and the Books

IN a previous chapter we dealt with the question of the Mosaic authorship of the Pentateuch in a general way. We now desire to go a step farther, and to make a few inquiries relating to a few books of the Pentateuch. Some questions will be asked that can not be ignored or answered (in a general way) with a sort of blanket reply. The first of these books is

Genesis. — Did Jesus teach anything which fairly implies that Moses knew the Book of Genesis? In Mark's Gospel, chapter x, 2–6, we read:

> And the Pharisees came to him and asked him, Is it lawful for a man to put away his wife? tempting him. And he answered and said unto them, What did

> Moses command you? And they said, Moses suffered to write a bill of divorcement, and to put her away. And Jesus answered and said unto them, For the hardness of your heart he wrote you this precept. But from the beginning of the creation God made them male and female. For this same cause shall a man leave his father and his mother, and cleave to his wife.

Without dwelling on the interesting fact that in the verses cited our Lord quotes passages from the first and second chapters of Genesis, which chapters critics affirm belong to two different documents written at wide intervals of time from each other, as if they were of only one document, we may notice the statement that Moses " For the hardness of your heart wrote you this precept."

What does this statement, without any forcing of texts, fairly imply? It implies, we think, *first*, that Moses did write the statute on divorce in the

Deuteronomic Code; and *second*, which is the point here, that when he wrote it, he knew that another law, ancient law, was in existence which was not in harmony with his "*precept.*"

For making his precept a law in Israel, notwithstanding its opposition to a law as ancient as the creation of man, Moses had a valid reason, the "*hardness*" of the people's heart for whom he was legislating. Now observe, in Matthew we read: "Moses *suffered* you to put away your wives." There were hesitancy, questions of expediency, restraint of some character or other from some source; and the inference is, If it were not for "the hardness of your heart," Moses would not have "*suffered*" that precept to become a law in Israel. Why not? Because "it was not so at the beginning," and Moses knew it was out of harmony with the Divine idea. But if the Book of Genesis was not in existence, if Moses did not know anything of it, how did he know that the new precept was *not* in accordance with the original relation of man and wife? The statement that Moses "*suffered*" the indulgence of divorce indicates that he did have personal knowledge of the Divine idea in Genesis concerning the relation binding on man and wife. Otherwise, how could he "*suffer*" on account of heart "*hardness*" a departure from a law or custom of the existence of which he was ignorant? The Book of Genesis, then, was in existence in the days of Moses; for if not, there was no reason for his protesting permission. He does not "*suffer*" other laws—he enacts them; for they are not in violation of any other law written or unwritten. But this one is; hence the statement of our Lord. It can not be denied that, in the history of man's creation as recorded in Genesis, Moses recognized the Divine will relating to marriage; and that only the "hardness" of the people induced him to "*suffer*" divorce under special limitation.

The Book of Genesis was not only in existence in the days of Moses, but if that be granted—and we see no way to conclude otherwise—we are led to infer that he was the author of it, or the compiler of its narratives; for he only stands out in that remote age as the religious leader, lawgiver, and father of his nation. What the Pyramids of Egypt were to other structures, he was to all men then living.

Exodus.—What evidence is there that Moses wrote the Book

of Exodus? It may be necessary in this case to remind the reader that the five books of Moses, or the Pentateuch, are called in the Hebrew Canon, or accepted list of sacred books having Divine authority, "*The Book of the Law*," or simply "*The Law.*" We read of *The Book of the Law*, Deut. xxxi, 26; see also Joshua i, 8; viii, 34; 2 Kings xxii, 8, 11; 2 Chron. xxxiv, 15; Neh. viii, 1; ix, 3. Sometimes they are designated "*The Book of Moses*," as in 2 Chron. xxv, 4; xxxv, 12; see also Ezra vi, 18; Neh. xiii, 1.

By these titles the Pentateuch was known to the ancient Hebrews; and down to the time of Christ, and since, among the Jews, the Book of Moses was understood to stand for and include the five books of Moses, which by us

Christians are called the Pentateuch.

Now, in Mark xii, 26, we read:

> And as touching the dead, that they rise; have ye not read in the Book of Moses, how in the bush God spake unto him, saying, etc.

The account of this event in the life of Moses is found in the Book of Exodus only. The Book of Exodus, then, is a book of Moses; and by our Lord is so named and accepted. The occasion for the reference to this book was an attempt on the part of some of the Sadducean party to puzzle our Lord by one of the stock objections with which they annoyed the Pharisees concerning their doctrine of the resurrection. "*Master*," they said, as they proceeded to state their ingenious problem, "*Master, Moses wrote unto us, if any man's brother die having a wife,*" etc. The law of Moses which they quoted is written in Deuteronomy xxv, 5. Let us observe, the Divine Teacher, recognizing the fact that these Sadducees accepted the inspiration of the Pentateuch only, does not go outside the Pentateuch. Since they quoted Moses to overthrow the doctrine of the resurrection, he would also quote Moses to establish what they would destroy.

Now the critics concede that Moses wrote the Code in Deuteronomy in which the above law is found. But if Moses was *not* the author of the Book of Exodus, how could our Lord have quoted Moses out of Exodus to defend Moses in Deuteronomy? Moses, say the critics, was not the author of Exodus, and was therefore not responsible for its teachings; but he was the author of the Deuteronomic Code, and so here is Christ putting a fictitious author to defend a real author. Moses did not teach what was attributed to him by our Lord; but Jesus drew his own conclusions from what some unknown author said about Moses, and the Sadducean problem was therefore not fairly answered. Are we ready for such conclusions? How can we avoid them? There is only one logical way to avoid them, and that is by believing that Moses did actually write the Book of Exodus, as is evident from the fact that Christ ascribed the authorship of Exodus to the *same person* to whom he and the Sadducees, and also modern critics, ascribed the authorship of the Deuteronomic Code.

We are aware, of course, that the critics accept the fact that Christ accepted the views of the

Old Testament "current about him;" but are they willing to accept the consequences of that statement? The Sadducees quoted an indisputable author as authority for a certain law, from which law they drew arguments tending to establish their belief. Christ wishes to show them their error, and to do this he quotes a book which they accepted as inspired, written by the same author they quoted. But the book he quoted was not written by that same author. Does not radical criticism, then, show that in reality the Sadducees had the better of the argument; that it was only their ignorance of the fact that Moses was not the author of Exodus that prevented them from replying, "Your answer is not valid, for Moses did not write that book, and you can not quote the authority of Moses, in whom we believe, for a doctrine which he nowhere taught?" Are the critics willing to accept the consequences of their conclusions?

That our Lord believed in the Mosaic authorship of Exodus is further seen in Luke's account of this same circumstance:

> Now that the dead are raised, even Moses shewed at the bush, when he calleth the Lord the God of Abraham, and the God of Isaac, and the God of Jacob. (Luke xx, 37.)

When we turn to the original account in Ex. iii, 6, we read that these appellations were spoken by God himself of himself, and not by Moses. But our Lord attributes these names to Moses on the ground that *he recorded* them; that he was the historian of the events written in the Book of Exodus. The only reply that a thoroughgoing critic can make to this is a re-statement of the limitations of our Lord's knowledge, which is only saying that Christ was mistaken.

Leviticus. — Who wrote the Book of Leviticus? This question is in our appeal to the Master, and his statement for us, at least, has the value of finality. In Matt. viii, there is the record of Christ healing a leper:

> And Jesus saith unto him, See thou tell no man; but go thy way, shew thyself to the priest, and offer the gift that Moses commanded, for a testimony unto them.

The Law of the Leper is found in Leviticus xiv, and the gifts to be offered are mentioned in verses 10, 21, 22. This law, Christ said, was commanded by Moses; that is, Moses wrote the law. Over against all theories of ritual development in national history insisted upon by radical critics, there stands this expressed statement of our Lord. When we turn to Leviticus at the Law of the Leper we find this: *"And the Lord spake unto Moses saying, This shall be the Law of the Leper in the day of his cleansing."* Not to unknown authors was this law given, but to a well-known, definite personage — to Moses. The lawgiver, then, according to the law-chapter itself, was the author, not necessarily the one actually holding the pen, but the author, no matter how many scribes he employed to do the mechanical work of the Book of Leviticus. These laws could not have originated in later ages without the enactors and scribes of these laws being guilty of an historical falsehood. That it was a practice in ancient times to ascribe certain writings to eminent characters in order that they might have the authority and influence which such characters could give them is not applicable here, unless it can be shown, as it has not been, that such was the practice among the Hebrews in floating their sacred books. To say that Jehovah spoke to Moses the contents of a book when that book originated, as the author would know it did, ages after the death of Moses, is a crime of which no Hebrew could be guilty. Jehovah was too real a God for a Hebrew to do that.

Further, if we accept the theory of historical falsehood we must also believe that that falsehood and many others like it were all continued under the protection of Divine Providence down to the time of Christ, when they deceived *him*, and on to our day. Now, it is much more rational to **believe that there is no historical** falsehood in the case. It is better to believe this than it is to believe that God would have protected that falsehood in protecting his Word; that Christ was deceived by it; and that from his day until now the whole world has been falsely led to believe that God had spoken these statutes to Moses. It is really too much of a burden to place on human credulity. I would rather believe that our critics are mistaken. Christ said Moses commanded certain laws. I turn to those laws, they are in Leviticus; *Moses, therefore, wrote Leviticus.*

Numbers.—For the Book of Numbers there is no express testimony of the Lord such as we find for the other Books of the Pentateuch, nor, judging from the subject matter of that book, should we expect to find any. The Book of Numbers, however, was regarded by the Lord as of Mosaic origin; for it was included among the books which were always known as the Book of the Law, the Book of Moses.

Deuteronomy.—That our Lord taught this book to be the work of Moses, and not of some scribe of after ages, is evident from a study of many passages, a few of which we notice—Matt. xix, 7, 8; John vii, 19, 24; viii, 5, 7:

> They say unto him, Why did Moses then command to give a writing of divorcement? etc. (Matt. xix, 7, 8.)

This text would lead us pretty much over the same ground we have already traversed in our notes on Genesis. We may remark, however, that this text shows a desire on the part of the Pharisees to confound our Lord by setting Moses against Moses. They think they see a contradiction between Genesis i, 27; v, 2, which our Lord quoted, and Deuteronomy xxiv, 1. Had Moses not written Deuteronomy, the seeming riddle of the Pharisees could be shown to be no riddle at all, and the statement of the eminent critic, Canon Driver, of Oxford, that "there is no record of the question whether a particular portion of the Old Testament was written by Moses, or Daniel, or Isaiah, having been ever submitted to him," could not have been so easily answered.

Christ, in reply to his interlocutors, quotes a passage from the Book of Genesis, which they accepted as being from Moses. Immediately they respond, "Why did Moses then command to give a writing of divorcement?" Our Lord, say the conclusions of the critics, could have replied: "Moses was not the author of Deuteronomy. It belongs to the age of

King Josiah, and is not to be quoted against the primal law of God." But instead of repudiating the Mosaic authorship of Deuteronomy, our Lord expressly confirms it; and not only so, but in addition he *gives the reason* why Moses wrote the Law of Divorce: "Moses, *because of the hardness of your hearts*, suffered you to put away your wives; but from the beginning it was not so."

The contention of Dr. Briggs and of Professor Gore that because of the limitations of our Lord's humanity he did not know who wrote Deuteronomy, and of Canon Driver that our Lord simply accepted the opinions "current about him," seems, in the presence of this text, very much like a futile threshing of the atmosphere. *Why* Moses gave that law was never known until Christ revealed it, and it certainly was not possible for any one to have discovered it with any assurance of certainty. But if Christ knew what no mortal man did know—*i. e., why that law was given*—did he not know whether or no Moses was the author of that law? If our Lord did not know, and could not have known, who the author was, how could he have known *the reason* for the law?

Take another passage, John vii, 19:

> Did not Moses give you the law, and yet none of you keepeth the law?

In Deuteronomy xxxiii, 4, we find the people saying the same, "Moses commanded us a law." Christ declares that Moses gave the law, which of course includes all the laws in Deuteronomy. One of these laws was against murder. Our Lord says: "None of you keepeth the law. Why go ye about to kill me?" This law, the whole Book of the Law, has for its author Moses; and the depth of moral turpitude seen in the desires of Christ's enemies lies in their double condemnation, that, in addition to intentional murder, they were hypocritical professors of obedience to the laws of Moses. But bad as these men were, if Moses was not the author of these laws, could they be justly condemned for not keeping the laws of Moses?

Again, in John viii, 5, we read, in the case of the woman who found a defender in her Judge:

> Now Moses in the law commanded us that such should be stoned: but what sayest thou?

The law is recorded in Leviticus xx, 20, and in Deuteronomy xxii, 22. Our blessed Lord does not question the authority of the law;

for he knows its Divine origin. He does not invalidate the Book of Deuteronomy by denying its Mosaic authorship, and as therefore without authority unless indorsed in this particular by Roman civil law, with which an execution by the public would be in conflict; for the power of capital punishment had been taken away from the Jewish leaders. On the contrary, since his interlocutors had quoted to him the law, he also, seemingly on the principle that he who comes into court, human or Divine, must come with clean hands, would quote from the Book of the Law. But of all the books in the Bible, he refers to the very book in which their legal precept is recorded, the Book of Deuteronomy: "The hands of the witnesses shall be first upon him to put him to death, and afterward the hands of all the people." (Deut. xvii, 7.)

These are the Five Books of Moses, and such is the testimony of our Lord to their Mosaic authorship. Nowhere have we consciously forced any passage out of its obvious meaning, nor can it be said that our argument is "an ever-widening spiral *ergo* from the narrow aperture of single texts." The testimony of our Lord is abundant, and the only reply that the critics can make is, that either he did not know, did not care, or that he was mistaken.

CHAPTER VI

Reconciliation

WE have reached our conclusion. The verdict, based on the evidence presented, will be, we assume, that Christ has spoken, and that Moses was the author of the Pentateuch.

Now, what? What will be the, at least, apparent logical consequences of such a verdict? What, to be explicit, would be the effect on Biblical science in general if the results of our investigations were accepted and honestly applied in the study of Biblical criticism?

We suppose that the ultra-conservative would gladly consider it as a perpetual injunction against Higher Criticism. The enthusiastic critic, devoted to the study of historic truth regardless of traditions and baseless notions, would look upon it as the senseless enemy of all true progress. To the former, the verdict would be delightfully satisfactory, since all vexatious problems of contradictory statements, textual emendations, editorial interpolations; all questions of authorship, authenticity, and genuineness,— would be settled for him without any labor, anxiety, or doubt on his part. To the latter, it would be as the cry of the Israelites for the fleshpots of Egypt. Better the wilderness, he thinks, with its dangers and difficulties, but with its progress also toward Canaan, than lentils and slavery in Goshen. He will never retreat. Nothing is more exasperating to the genuine searcher for truth than the attempt to solve serious problems by a peremptory and reactionary "Thus saith the Lord!" For, to change a little the phraseology of an English writer of an earlier day, of all the cants which are canted in this canting world, while the cant of criticism may be the worst, the cant of mistaken piety is the most tormenting.

But is it not possible that the conclusions we have reached may not, after all, be productive of such baneful results? The fear of the critic, we are inclined to think, is groundless; and the satisfaction of the conservative may be, in its continuance, as the dew of the morning. The statements of our Lord concerning the authorship of the Pentateuch may not render so worthless the labors of Biblical critics, or bar the open path of progress so completely, as some imagine. We can appeal to Christ, and we may gladly accept his statements, and still be loyal, we believe, to the principles and methods of Higher Criticism. In other words, we do not believe it is necessary to ignore the declarations of Christ in order to prosecute scientifically our study of the Bible. No statement of the Lord that Moses was the author of any book rivets us down to the unreasonable belief that Moses sat, pen in hand, and originally wrote every word in that book as we now have it. Such an extreme view as that is as ridiculous as the notion that Moses was not an author at all. Putting Scripture on the rack, and forcing it to speak as we desire, is an unholy use of the Sacred Oracle. Neither men nor Scriptures should be placed on the rack or broken on the wheel over this contention; for we can all see how Paul could certainly be the author of the Epistle to the Romans, even if Tertius did write it (Rom. xvi, 22), and Moses could also have been an author, although others edited and added to his work in after centuries.

Jesus knew the Scriptures. No one denies that, and it would be presumption to prove it. We neither assume nor imagine that he studied them according to the principles and methods of modern criticism. But that he was ignorant of any question ever being raised concerning the authorship of certain books and the authority of others, we do not believe; for we do not suppose that any educated person from Dan to Beersheba was ignorant of the debates that once animated the theological schools of the great Rabbins Hillel and Schammai.

Now, many passages held as proof by modern critics that Moses did not write the Pentateuch must surely have been as well known to the Great Teacher as they are to us; and, from the nature of the case and the constitution of the human mind, they must have awakened thought in him as to their authorship as they do in us. Jesus, we suppose, knew that Moses did not write Deuteronomy xxxiv, 5-12. Did our Lord never read Gen. xii, 6; xiii, 7—"The Canaanite was then in the land"—and did it never occur to him, as it has occurred to us, that that statement must have been written at a time when the Canaanite was *not* in the land? In Gen. xiv, 14, and in Deut. xxiv, 1, as we have seen, mention is made of a place called Dan, a name not given to the town till long after the days of

Moses, as is recorded in Judges xviii, 29. Did our Lord in his study of Holy Scripture never read those passages? A similar instance is furnished by a comparison of Gen. xiii, 8, with Joshua xiv, 15; xv, 13. Again, in Gen. xxxvi, 31, it is written: "And these are the kings that reigned in the land of Edom before there reigned any king over the children of Israel." Could that have been written in the days of Moses, and did our Lord never read it? Exodus xvi, 35, was not written by Moses, nor can we bring ourselves to believe that he wrote Deut. ii, 22; iii, 14; x, 8, and other passages in which we find the phrase "unto this day." These texts have always been in the Bible; their difficulties are no new, startling discovery, resulting from the extraordinary ingenuity of modern criticism; for it has never required exceptional critical skill to discover what ordinary reading will reveal, and we must give the Lord some credit as a careful student of the Holy Word. Indeed, we think very few difficulties, discrepancies, or contradictions in the old Bible, so conspicuously paraded by rationalistic critics of extreme type, were unknown to him who once said to the rationalists of his day, "Search the Scriptures!" And yet this same Jesus said, "Moses wrote."

Nothing, then, that can set aside that reiterated statement— not the fact that certain books have texts imbedded in them which Moses could not have written, for as a student of the Sacred Books Christ knew that; not the fact that therefore they must have been edited and added to by another hand, for that also is evident; nor even the possible fact that large sections closely related to identical subjects originally treated, and out of which they were developed, as was perhaps the priestly Code in Leviticus out of the less elaborate Code in Deuteronomy, for addition to a work does not destroy the claim of the original author,— none of these facts invalidate the words of Christ, nor, on the other hand, do these words bar the progress of true Biblical study, or render nugatory the conclusions of scholars who are not the willing victims of preconceived opinions. We can still be students of Biblical criticism, it would seem, without surrendering to the premature *dicta* of Kuenen and Welhausen, and the whole crowd of Hegelian dreamers, who base criticism on philosophy, and philosophy on imagination.

We can also be progressive students of the Word without adopting the views of Professors Driver, Gore, and others of like teaching, who are evidently unwilling to grant to the profoundest student of the Word of God that ever looked into its pages the critical acumen, even of the Rabbins, who disputed in the schools in the generation preceding him. Even when but a mere boy of twelve years he was once found in the company of Israel's teachers, "hearing them and asking them questions, and all that heard him were astonished at his understanding and answers." (Luke ii, 46, 47.) From that time till he entered formally upon his ministry, eighteen years of study and meditation elapsed, and we fail to see why Omniscience was necessary to the student Jesus before he could have an opinion on the Mosaic authorship of the Pentateuch, but is not necessary to our modern critics.

We gladly admit that the accumulated wisdom of the past, the knowledge and experience of the race, have widened immeasurably the horizon of every laborious thinker, and that the student of history or of science is now in possession of facts not obtainable by men of ancient days without the miraculous gift of superhuman knowledge.

But such an admission must not be pushed too far. It may be accepted as true with reference to the ever-enlarging domain of the physical sciences, but it can not be true if it is forced to include the fields of philosophy and religion. Neither Plato nor Aristotle was favored with omniscience, and yet neither Kant, nor Descartes, nor Hegel has wholly superseded those immortal thinkers. Plato rules a larger empire to-day than ever. Biblical critics depend wholly on the internal evidence of the several books of the Bible for their conclusions; but this evidence— we mean the discrepancies above cited—was also in the Bible that Christ read, and from which he quoted, and the discrepancies were doubtless just as clear to him as they are to us. But if omniscience was not a necessary prerequisition to either Plato or Aristotle, to Kant or to Hegel, and is not a *sine qua non* to the modern student of Biblical criticism, why should it have been necessary to the Great Teacher, Christ Jesus? The difference between the subjects—one philosophy and the other Scripture—will not afford any sure ground for the necessity. Finally, Christ said Moses wrote; the Pentateuch itself proves that Moses could not have written it as it now is; Christ therefore could not have meant that Moses wrote it as it now is; for the evidence was before him as it is before us; and the office, therefore, of a genuine Higher Criticism is not to ignore the words of Christ, but to show us truly what Moses did write.

We may well believe that, as between religion and true science there is no feud, so between Christ and genuine criticism there is no conflict.

www.ingramcontent.com/pod-product-compliance
Lightning Source LLC
Chambersburg PA
CBHW020307090426
42735CB00009B/1260